1/24/19

UFOs

ARE ALIEN AIRCRAFT OVERHEAD?

MEGAN BORGERT-SPANIOL

**Checkerboard
Library**

An Imprint of Abdo Publishing
abdopublishing.com

ABDOPUBLISHING.COM

Published by Abdo Publishing, a division of ABDO, PO Box 398166, Minneapolis, Minnesota 55439.
Copyright © 2019 by Abdo Consulting Group, Inc. International copyrights reserved in all countries.
No part of this book may be reproduced in any form without written permission from the publisher.
Checkerboard Library™ is a trademark and logo of Abdo Publishing.

Printed in the United States of America, North Mankato, Minnesota
052018
092018

Design: Emily O'Malley, Mighty Media, Inc.
Production: Mighty Media, Inc.
Editor: Jessie Alkire
Cover Photographs: Shutterstock
Interior Photographs: Alamy, pp. 11, 17; AP Images, pp. 5, 18, 19, 25, 28 (top); iStockphoto, pp. 7,
29 (bottom); Shutterstock, pp. 8, 15, 21, 27, 28 (bottom), 29 (top); Wikimedia Commons, pp. 13, 23,
28 (middle)

Library of Congress Control Number: 2017961636

Publisher's Cataloging-in-Publication Data
Names: Borgert-Spaniol, Megan, author.
Title: UFOs: Are alien aircraft overhead? / by Megan Borgert-Spaniol.
Other titles: Are alien aircraft overhead?
Description: Minneapolis, Minnesota : Abdo Publishing, 2019. | Series: Science fact or
     science fiction? | Includes online resources and index.
Identifiers: ISBN 9781532115424 (lib.bdg.) | ISBN 9781532156144 (ebook)
Subjects: LCSH: Unidentified flying objects--Juvenile literature. | Extraterrestrial beings-
     -Juvenile literature. | Life on other planets--Juvenile literature. | Outer space--
     Exploration--Juvenile literature. | Science fiction in science education--Juvenile
     literature.
Classification: DDC 001.942--dc23

CONTENTS

FLYING SAUCERS!

On June 24, 1947, pilot Kenneth Arnold was flying his small plane above the state of Washington. The sky was clear as Arnold soared 9,200 feet (2,804 m) above the ground. Suddenly, a bright light hit the plane. Arnold looked in the direction the light came from. He was shocked at what he saw!

Nine aircraft flew past Arnold. They were moving in a *V*-shaped formation. But the mysterious aircraft didn't have wings and tails like most aircraft. One of the objects was **crescent**-shaped and the others were circular. They moved together at great speed. Arnold guessed the aircraft were traveling about 1,700 miles per hour (2,736 kmh). He had never seen anything like them!

Later, Arnold described the objects to the press. He said the objects moved like saucers skipping across water. Newspapers mistakenly reported that the objects were shaped like saucers. From then on, such objects were often called "flying saucers."

Kenneth Arnold's story was a national headline. An investigation determined that Arnold saw a mirage or disk-shaped clouds.

Arnold thought the objects might have been new military aircraft. But the US War Department thought Arnold had imagined the aircraft. As Arnold's story spread, other witnesses reported seeing similar aircraft. What were these unidentified objects, and where did they come from?

Kenneth Arnold was unable to identify the flying objects he had seen that June day. And many other reported objects have been unexplainable too. Such objects are known as Unidentified Flying Objects, or UFOs. The term *UFO* can apply to any flying object that hasn't been identified.

UFOs have been spotted for centuries! Long ago, these objects were often linked to angels, demons, and other supernatural beings. Since more modern times, UFOs have been widely associated with **extraterrestrial** visitors.

Official investigations have found common characteristics among UFO sightings. For example, many sighted UFOs are shaped like disks or saucers. Others are shaped like cigars or **torpedoes**. UFOs also commonly appear as hovering balloon-shaped objects or even moving balls of light.

There are also common patterns in the way UFOs have been reported to move. Many witnesses have claimed to see multiple UFOs flying in certain formations. The objects are often reported to make unnatural or sudden movements. Many UFOs are said to glide through the air without making a single sound!

Most UFO sightings occur in the United States. But Canada, Sweden, Denmark, the United Kingdom, and other countries have kept UFO sighting records too.

A phenomenon related to UFOs is crop circles. These are mysterious circular patterns in fields. Many people think this happens because of a UFO landing!

Many reports describe more than just a UFO sighting. Some describe physical evidence of the UFO. Witnesses have claimed to find vegetation flattened, burned, or broken by UFOs. Researchers have found plants that underwent strange chemical changes at reported UFO landing sites. Scientists think this could have been caused by **radiation** from a UFO or some other mysterious source! But many cases have scientific reasons, such as lightning.

UFOs have also been reported to have physical effects on humans. UFO witnesses have noted certain **symptoms**. Some people have experienced burns, blisters, and stomach pain. Others were temporarily deaf or had memory loss. Sometimes these symptoms lasted for years.

The United States, Canada, and other countries have kept records of UFO sightings over many years. The US military launched studies to explain UFOs. But some reports remain unexplained. Such unsolved mysteries leave many people wondering, are alien aircraft overhead?

FOR REAL?

US Presidents Jimmy Carter and Ronald Reagan have reported seeing UFOs. Other famous UFO spotters include musician John Lennon and NASA astronaut Buzz Aldrin.

HISTORY OF UFOs

Humans have been spotting UFOs for thousands of years. Egyptians, Greeks, and other ancient people referenced sightings in artwork and literature. These works described strange lights and objects in the sky. Such sightings continued through the **Middle Ages**.

In the 1890s, reports of cigar-shaped aircraft came in across the United States. The so-called "airships" **amazed** witnesses from across the United States. Airplanes weren't invented yet, so the airships were a mystery. Some believed these aircraft had **extraterrestrial** origins.

The mid-1900s marked the beginning of modern UFO sightings. Arnold's experience in 1947 was the first well-known sighting. After that, more and more sightings were reported. Magazines and newspapers helped fuel a new American fascination with UFOs.

The US Air Force decided to investigate UFO sightings. Its longest investigation began in 1952. It was called

Members of Project Blue Book's staff

Project Blue Book. Over 17 years, Project Blue Book researchers gathered reports of more than 12,000 UFO sightings and events.

The US government also established a panel of scientists to investigate UFOs. The panel was headed by **physicist** H.P. Robertson. In January 1953, the Robertson Panel reviewed UFO sighting data, films, and images.

The panel didn't find any evidence of alien connections. It concluded that 90 percent of UFO sightings were caused by human-made objects or common atmospheric events. These included bright stars and planets, meteors, balloons, and other kinds of aircraft.

In 1966, another panel of scientists was formed to investigate Project Blue Book data. Physicist Edward U. Condon led this committee. The panel released the Condon Report in 1968. The report's findings were similar to those of the Robertson Panel. Its writers concluded that further UFO studies were not necessary.

The year after the Condon Report came out, the US Air Force ended Project Blue Book. But some

FOR REAL?

In April 1897, an **alleged** UFO crash took place in Aurora, Texas. Witnesses reportedly uncovered the body of the aircraft's pilot. They claimed the pilot did not look human!

scientists believed UFOs were still worth studying. While most UFO sightings could be explained, some were still mysteries. Meanwhile, many Americans thought the government was covering up the truth. They believed authorities were hiding evidence of **extraterrestrial** UFOs. Such **conspiracy theories** still exist today!

The Condon Report studied UFO images from McMinnville, Oregon. The Condon Report couldn't explain these images!

One of the most famous UFO incidents took place outside Roswell, New Mexico, in July 1947. A rancher named Mac Brazel was crossing his land when he noticed something unusual. Scraps of metal, plastic, and other debris were scattered over the desert. Brazel alerted Roswell police officers to what he had found. The police notified the US Air Force.

On July 8, a Roswell newspaper broke the story. It reported that a flying saucer had been found on Brazel's ranch. The next day, a US Air Force official announced that the debris was from a crashed weather balloon. But some people believed this was a cover-up. They thought the debris was from a crashed UFO from outer space.

It wasn't until 50 years later that the truth came out. The debris in Roswell wasn't from a weather balloon after all. It had been from a secret US military mission called Project Mogul. The project used high-altitude balloons to detect nuclear testing in the Soviet Union.

Roswell's International UFO Museum and Research Center has many exhibits on spacecraft and life-size alien models!

The Air Force **declassified** most of its Project Mogul files in the 1990s. The public finally knew the truth about Roswell. But many people are still **skeptical** of the government's explanation. They continue to think a UFO crashed at Roswell. Today, the city is home to the International UFO Museum and Research Center. It also hosts an annual UFO festival!

15

TAKEN!

UFO reports sometimes involve more than strange sights or wreckage. Over the years, many people have claimed to meet **extraterrestrial** beings inside UFOs! These reports are often easy to prove wrong. Many reports come from unstable people or people seeking fame. But some reports come from trustworthy individuals. These cases are harder to explain.

One such case occurred in September 1961. Betty and Barney Hill were driving through the New Hampshire mountains when they spotted something behind them. It was a UFO! The cigar-shaped craft was following them closely. Two hours later, the Hills found themselves 35 miles (56 km) from where they'd seen the UFO. But they had no memory of how they got there.

FOR REAL?

The Hills described their **abductors** as short, bald beings with pear-shaped heads and slanted eyes. This is a common description of aliens today.

Betty and Barney Hill remembered undergoing medical and scientific tests aboard a UFO. Aliens then hypnotized the couple so they wouldn't remember the experience.

After this event, the Hills experienced nightmares and mental distress. In 1964, the couple decided to be **hypnotized**. They thought this might help them remember what happened during those forgotten hours. It seemed to work. Under hypnosis, the Hills described being taken aboard a spacecraft by aliens!

Vickie Landrum had a similar UFO incident to the Hills's. She and two others experienced blisters, headaches, and pain after encountering a diamond-shaped UFO.

The Hills's story was the first widely reported UFO **abduction** case. It sparked a public fascination with alien abduction. The couple was portrayed in the 1975 TV movie *The UFO Incident*. Years later in 2011, New Hampshire placed a historical highway marker where the Hills saw the UFO. But the debate continues. Were the Hills's memories of alien abduction real?

Names:

- Hill, Barney
- Hill, Betty

Incident Date and Location:

- September 19 to September 20, 1961
- White Mountains, New Hampshire, near Indian Head Resort

Claims:

- Encounter with cigar-shaped UFO
- Sighting of human-like figures through windows of UFO
- Two hours of memory loss after sighting

Evidence:

- Malfunction of Hills's watches
- Multiple tears in Betty's dress
- Unexplained scrapes on Barney's shoe
- Shiny circles on trunk of car
- Memories of **abduction** during **hypnosis**

Status:

UNSOLVED

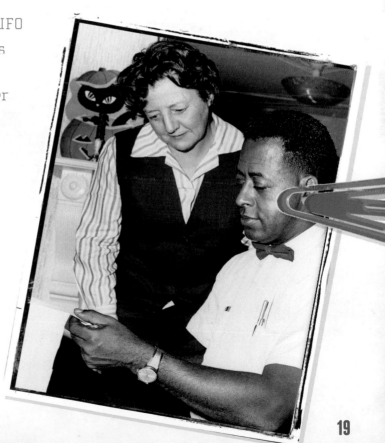

Many who believe in extraterrestrial visitors point to Area 51 as evidence. Area 51 is a US military facility in the remote Nevada desert. For many years, no one knew what activities went on at this secretive base. Since the 1950s, many UFO sightings have been reported in the area. This led to a popular belief that Area 51 is used for UFO and alien investigations.

In 1989, **physicist** Robert Lazar claimed these beliefs were true. Lazar said he had studied alien spacecraft while working at Area 51. Some people called Lazar's story a hoax. Others believed him.

Lazar's claim brought international attention to Area 51. It also fueled **conspiracy theories** about government cover-ups. Alien visitors became a popular topic of entertainment in the 1990s. The popular TV series *The X-Files* followed two agents uncovering secrets about extraterrestrials. In 1997, the comedy movie *Men in Black* featured agents in charge of policing aliens on Earth.

WARNING

Restricted Area

It is unlawful to enter this area without permission of the Installation Commander.
Sec. 21, Internal Security Act of 1950, 50 U.S.C. 797

While on this Installation all personnel and the property under their control are subject to search.

Use of deadly force authorized.

WARNING!

NO TRESPASSING
AUTHORITY N.R.S. 207-200
MAXIMUM PUNISHMENT: $1000 FINE
SIX MONTHS IMPRISMENT
OR BOTH
STRICTLY ENFORCED

PHOTOGRAPHY
OF THIS AREA
IS PROHIBITED
18-6-795

WARNING

MILITARY INSTALLATION

IT IS UNLAWFUL TO ENTER THIS INSTALLATION WITHOUT
THE WRITTEN PERMISSION OF THE INSTALLATION COMMANDER.

INSTALLATION COMMANDER
AUTHORITY: Internal Security Act, 50
U.S.C. 797
PUNISHMENT: Up to one year imprisonment
and $5,000. fine.

Area 51 has strict security restrictions. It is patrolled by security guards.
There are also sensors that detect human movement!

In 2013, the US government declassified information about Area 51. It revealed that Area 51 was a testing site for the U-2 spy plane in the 1950s. The U-2 could fly higher than any known commercial and military aircraft of the time. Many sighted UFOs were actually the unfamiliar U-2 plane.

Over the years, many types of military aircraft have been tested at Area 51. The facility is still used today! But these tests are classified, so the government can't reveal the aircraft's real identities. Many UFO sightings in the Soviet Union and China also resulted from secret aircraft testing.

Spy planes, weather balloons, and other human-made objects account for many UFO sightings. Atmospheric **phenomena** can also look like UFOs. For example, disk-shaped clouds have been known to trick viewers. Haze, fog, and natural light displays called auroras can also trick the eye.

Some UFOs really are from beyond Earth. But
they're not related to aliens. Meteors shoot into Earth's
atmosphere from outer space. Bright stars can appear to
move too. And the planet Venus often sits close to the
horizon like a hovering UFO.

The U-2 plane could fly 70,000 feet (21,336 m) up in the air.
This was much higher than other aircraft could fly at the time.

There are many possible explanations for UFO sightings. But can claims of alien **abduction** be explained as easily? Some experts think so.

Psychologists link many abduction stories to sleep **paralysis**. This condition occurs while a person is waking up or falling asleep. It makes an individual unable to move. People with sleep paralysis often **hallucinate**. They imagine seeing, hearing, or feeling another presence that isn't really there.

A person's memory can also be imagined or altered. Like Betty and Barney Hill, many people recall alien abductions while under **hypnosis**. But psychologists note that hypnosis can uncover memories of both real and imagined events.

FOR REAL?

In 1995, two men released a video of an alien body being examined. They claimed the alien was from the Roswell crash of 1947. They later admitted the video was a hoax.

Charles Hickson told a story of alien abduction in 1973. But some have suggested that Hickson experienced a hypnagogic state. This is a state between being awake and sleeping.

Some UFO sightings and alien **abductions** are neither real nor imagined. They are simply made up. People hoping to gain money or fame have shared fake stories, photos, and videos. With advances in digital **technology**, such hoaxes are easier than ever to create. However, people are also more **skeptical** of what they see in photos and videos today.

UFOs are still a topic of high interest today. In 2016, *The X-Files* returned after more than ten years off the air. That same year, the alien-encounter movie *Arrival* brought in more than $200 million in ticket sales. Meanwhile, witnesses in the sky and on the ground continue to report unidentified flying objects.

Despite continued sightings, UFO research is not well funded. Most governments and scientific institutions do not think UFOs are worth studying anymore. Organizations that investigate UFO sightings rely on member or public support. One such organization is the Center for UFO Studies (CUFOS) in Chicago, Illinois.

CUFOS was founded in 1973 by Dr. J. Allen Hynek, a former member of Project Blue Book. Hynek pushed for further study of UFO cases that could not be explained. He did not argue that UFOs were alien-made aircraft. But he was known for keeping an open mind to unexpected explanations.

Today, powerful telescopes allow scientists to search for planets that could support life. Are UFOs evidence that life exists outside our solar system? Or are they signs of something else entirely? In their quest for answers, researchers remain open to mystery.

In January 2016, Fox TV staff set up a crashed UFO in Los Angeles, California, to promote the new season of *The X-Files*!

XFiles   The Truth is Out There   #TheX

TIMELINE

1890s
Sightings of cigar-shaped "airships" are reported across the United States.

1947
Pilot Kenneth Arnold reports seeing strange objects flying in Washington.

1952
The longest US military investigation of UFOs begins. It is named Project Blue Book.

1961
Betty and Barney Hill encounter a UFO while driving in New Hampshire. They later have memories of alien abduction.

1968
The Condon Report concludes that further UFO studies are not necessary. Project Blue Book ends the next year.

1973
CUFOS is founded by Dr. J. Allen Hynek, a former member of Project Blue Book.

1989
Physicist Robert Lazar claims to have studied alien spacecraft while working at Area 51.

2013
A declassified report reveals that Area 51 had been a testing site for the U-2 spy plane.

2016
The popular TV series *The X-Files* returns after more than ten years off the air.

YOU DECIDE!

Are alien aircraft overhead? You decide!

- Explore UFO case studies at the library and online.
- Research sightings tracked by CUFOS, the Mutual UFO Network, and other organizations.
- Read articles about exoplanets and other deep-space research.
- And don't forget to keep an eye on the sky!

GLOSSARY

abduction—the taking of a person by force. A person who takes someone is an abductor.

alleged—said to be true but unproven.

amaze—to surprise or fill with wonder.

classified—kept from the public in order to protect national security. When something is no longer kept from the public, it is declassified.

conspiracy theory—belief that an event is caused by a secret plot.

crescent—a curved shape with pointed ends.

extraterrestrial—coming from beyond Earth. Someone or something from beyond Earth is also called an extraterrestrial.

hallucinate—to see, hear, or experience something that is not real.

hypnosis—a sleeplike state in which one is open to suggestion or direction. The act of putting someone in this state is to hypnotize.

Middle Ages—the period of history in Europe from about 500 CE to about 1500 CE.

paralysis—the loss of motion or feeling in a part of the body.

phenomenon—a fact or event that is rare or extraordinary.

physicist—a person who studies matter and energy and how they affect each other.

psychologist—a person who studies the science of the mind and behavior.

radiation—dangerous and powerful energy particles that are given off by something.

skeptical—having an attitude of doubt or disbelief.

symptom—a noticeable change in the normal working of the body.

technology—scientific tools or methods for doing tasks or solving problems.

torpedo—a submerged explosive.

ONLINE RESOURCES

Booklinks
NONFICTION NETWORK
FREE! ONLINE NONFICTION RESOURCES

To learn more about UFOs, visit **abdobooklinks.com**. These links are routinely monitored and updated to provide the most current information available.

INDEX